HISTORY
V·I·P

CHARLES
DARWIN

BRILLIANT
BIOGRAPHIES
of the
DEAD FAMOUS

Kay Barnham

First published in 2015 by Wayland
Copyright © Wayland 2015
All rights reserved.

Editor: Annabel Stones
Designer: Rocket Design (East Anglia) Ltd
Illustration: Emmanuel Cerisier, Beehive Illustration
Proofreader: Rebecca Clunes

Dewey number: 576.8'2'092-dc23
ISBN: 978 0 7502 8849 1
10 9 8 7 6 5 4 3 2 1

Wayland

An imprint of
Hachette Children's Group
Part of Hodder & Stoughton
Carmelite House
50 Victoria Embankment
London EC4Y 0DZ

An Hachette UK Company
www.hachette.co.uk
www.hachettechildrens.co.uk

Printed in China

Picture credits: iStockphoto: p19 © stockcam; SCIENCE PHOTO LIBRARY: p6 SCIENCE
SOURCE, p11, p23 NATURAL HISTORY MUSEUM, LONDON, p24 Science Source,
p29 EUROPEAN SPACE AGENCY; Shutterstock: p4 MarcelClemens, p5 Andrey Pavlov,
p12 sunsinger, p16 Nicku, p17 apiguide, p18 Don Fink, p21 Georgios Kollidas,
p25 right Everett Historical, p25 left IrinaK, p26 Everett Historical, p29 centre right
Giovanni G; Stefan Chabluk: p15. All graphic elements: Shutterstock.

CONTENTS

Introducing
CHARLES DARWIN

Why are there so many different types of animal? Where do they come from? And why do some animals become extinct?

In the nineteenth century, Charles Darwin worked out the answers to these questions. But then came the difficult part. He had to show everyone else that his explanations for how life evolves were right.

IN OTHER NEWS
CREATIONISM

The theory that a divine being created the universe and all species is known as Creationism. Creationists believe that the Earth and its creatures are the same today, as when they were first created.

Two hundred years ago, most people believed religious explanations of how the world and everything in it and around it were created. For example, the Bible tells how everything was created in seven days. But Darwin came up with a scientific explanation that challenged people's ideas about human and animal life.

Darwin was a naturalist, which is an animal and plant expert. He worked out why and how there are different species, or types, of animals and plants on the Earth. Then he spent a long time researching his findings. His ideas have changed the way humans think about themselves and the millions of other species alive today.

WHO WAS HE?

FULL NAME: Charles Robert Darwin
DATE OF BIRTH: 12 February 1809
LIVED: England
PARENTS: Robert and Susannah
SIBLINGS: five
JOB: naturalist and geologist
MARRIED: Emma Wedgwood
CHILDREN: 10 (seven survived childhood)
DIED: 19 April 1882

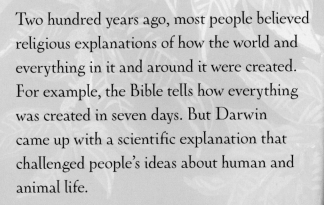

WHAT HE SAID

We can allow satellites, planets, suns, universe, nay whole systems of universes, to be governed by laws, but the smallest insect, we wish to be created at once by special act.

Charles Darwin

the BOY WHO LOVED NATURE

Charles Darwin came from a very distinguished family. One grandfather, Erasmus Darwin, was a physician and philosopher, while the other, Josiah Wedgwood, started the famous Wedgwood pottery company. Darwin's father, Robert Darwin, was a physician who treated the rich and famous. Charles Darwin was the fifth of six children, and the youngest son. His father's hobby was botany – the study of plants – and he encouraged Darwin's love of nature.

TRUE or FALSE?

DARWIN SHARED HIS FIRST PORTRAIT WITH A PLANT.

true He was already a naturalist, even in 1816. In this early portrait, seven-year-old Darwin and his younger sister, Catherine, are pictured holding plants.

Young Darwin eagerly read nature books and spent much of his time outdoors, in the fields near his Shrewsbury home. There, he collected his own specimens of plants and insects.

When Darwin was just eight, his mother died and his life changed. He was sent away to boarding school with his older brother. He didn't enjoy school at all. At every opportunity, he escaped the classroom to study nature instead.

Darwin loved to collect beetles. One day, he found two ground beetles, and picked them up, holding one in each hand. Then he spotted a third – a rare species called the crucifix ground beetle. Quickly, he popped one beetle between his teeth so he could pick up his new find. But the beetle promptly squirted a nasty juice into his mouth! Darwin spat it out in disgust and dropped the others.

WELL I NEVER!

Charles Darwin was born on the same day as US president, Abraham Lincoln (1809–1865).

the UNIVERSITY YEARS

In 1825, Darwin became a medical student at the University of Edinburgh. However, his attention kept wandering back to natural history. When he started to study medicine, Darwin found that the subject bored him. And, after watching an operation performed without anaesthetic, he found that surgery upset him too. So, he filled his time in other ways.

WHAT THEY SAID

You care for nothing but shooting, dogs, and rat-catching, and you will be a disgrace to yourself and all your family.

Charles Darwin's father (around 1828)

The Plinian Society was a club for students who were mad about natural history, just like Darwin. He joined in 1826 and became deeply involved with the society's activities. In 1827, he presented his own research into the black specks found in oyster shells, showing that these were skate leeches' eggs.

IN OTHER NEWS

THE WORLD'S FIRST COMPUTER

In 1823, Charles Babbage started to design his Difference Engine – an automatic mechanical calculator. It would be able to do a large number of calculations much faster than a human mathematician. It was never built. But Babbage's second design was produced. A working model of the Difference Engine No. 2 is displayed in the Science Museum in London.

Once his father realised that Darwin was neglecting his degree studies, he decided to do something about it. He sent him to Christ's College, Cambridge instead. Here, Darwin took theology – the study of God and religious beliefs. Darwin's father hoped that one day his son would become a parson. Yet once more, Darwin found it hard to focus on his degree. He rode horses, hunted and collected beetles. He also met and spent time with top naturalists. Among them was John Henslow, a botany professor who would be a key influence in the young Darwin's life.

TRUE or FALSE?

IN HIS SPARE TIME, DARWIN STUFFED ANIMALS.

true Darwin had a curious hobby when he was at Edinburgh University. He learned taxidermy – how to stuff animals.

At the last minute, Darwin decided to focus on his studies and passed his degree. He was expected to enter the church, but he stunned everyone by doing something completely different…

oyster shells

HMS BEAGLE

Rather than becoming a parson, Darwin travelled around the world. When he was given the opportunity to go on a two-year voyage on HMS *Beagle*, he jumped at the chance. Darwin's botany professor, John Henslow, had recommended him for a position on board the ship. If he took the job, Darwin would work as a naturalist and keep the ship's captain company too.

In the nineteenth century, maps were less detailed. So the main purpose of the HMS *Beagle's* voyage was to survey the coastline of the southern part of South America. The crew took measurements of shorelines, tides and currents. Better maps and information would make the coasts easier and safer for ships to navigate in the future.

The only drawback was that Darwin would have to pay all his own expenses. As he hadn't earned any money yet, that meant asking for his father's help. At first Robert Darwin wasn't keen; he thought it would be a total waste of his son's time. Luckily, he was persuaded otherwise and agreed to fund the voyage.

On 27 December 1831, HMS *Beagle* set sail.

HMS Beagle

Type of craft: Cherokee-class brig-sloop

Launched: 11 May 1820

Length: 27.5 metres

Capacity: in times of war, the ship could hold 120 people, but on Darwin's voyage, there were about 74 on board.

Crew: when the ship set sail in 1831, there was a surgeon, a draughtsman, a surveyor and a carpenter among the crew. And, of course, there was a naturalist.

WELL I NEVER!

In 1820, the HMS *Beagle* was the first ship to sail under old London Bridge as part of a procession of ships celebrating the coronation of George IV. And although Darwin's journey is known as the Voyage of the Beagle, this was actually the ship's second voyage. She sailed on two other surveying expeditions.

WHAT HE SAID

In conclusion, it appears that nothing can be more improving to a young naturalist, than a journey in distant countries.

Voyage of the Beagle *by Charles Darwin*

VOYAGE of the BEAGLE

The voyage didn't last two years, as originally planned. Instead, Darwin spent five years on board HMS *Beagle*. It became not just a surveying expedition, but a voyage of discovery too. The wonders Darwin saw made him think about the world and all its creatures in a totally different way.

WELL I NEVER!

Among the many species Darwin discovered on the Galápagos Islands was a bird with blue feet! The blue-footed booby is a long-winged seabird.

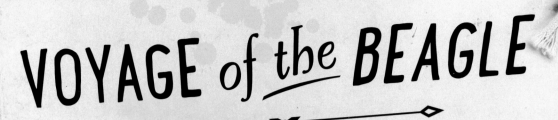

The huge fossils that he saw in Argentina made him keen to find out more about geology. He'd already read ideas about the way the Earth changes over time. When an earthquake in Chile shifted the landscape before his very eyes, Darwin was stunned.

Strange creatures fascinated him. On the Galápagos Islands in the Pacific Ocean, he saw giant tortoises and marine iguanas, unlike any he'd seen before. While in Australia, he saw koalas and kangaroos and wondered why they didn't live anywhere else in the world. Throughout his voyage, Darwin saw a huge variety landscapes. He examined coral reefs in Australia; marvelled at Table Mountain in South Africa; and visited jungles in South America.

Later, Darwin wrote all about his adventures in a book known today as *The Voyage of the Beagle*.

TRUE or FALSE?

DARWIN WAS A BRILLIANT SAILOR.

false Darwin was horribly seasick on board the HMS *Beagle*. The sickness started almost as soon as the ship set sail. By the time he reached the Bay of Biscay – the sea off the coasts of France and Spain – he said that he was 'wretchedly out of spirits and very sick'. He felt ill for the rest of the voyage.

FAME and FINDINGS

During the voyage, Darwin wrote regularly to John Henslow, telling him about his findings and his ideas. The professor, eager to share Darwin's exciting news, passed it on to a few naturalists. Word spread. And when he returned home in 1836, Darwin was a star — in the world of science, at least.

Now Darwin faced the same problem he'd had before setting sail on HMS *Beagle*: money. He wasn't linked to a university, which meant that he wouldn't be paid for being a scientist. He would have to fund himself, again. Luckily, his father stepped in once more with the money he needed.

Darwin was keen to examine the specimens he'd brought back with him from the expedition. But these were so many and so varied that he didn't have the knowledge or the time to look at them all. So he toured London, looking for experts who would share this massive task. They were only too glad to help.

Two months after the HMS *Beagle* had docked in Cornwall, England, Darwin began studying the journal that he'd kept during the voyage. He had a lot to write about.

★ Geological ★ Society of London

Founded in 1807, the Geological Society of London is the oldest geological society in the world. The UK society was formed so that geologists could meet, share and discuss new finds, and plan expeditions. They could also record what was already known about the science of geology so far, and what was yet to be discovered.

Darwin presented his first paper – on the subject of the South American landmass rising – to the Geological Society of London in January 1837. The geologists were so impressed that they made him a member the following month.

WELL I NEVER!

By the time he returned home from his voyage, Charles Darwin had actually circumnavigated the globe! Here's the route the HMS *Beagle* took.

15

DARWIN'S FINCHES

Of all the specimens that Darwin brought back from his voyage, his finches are among the most famous. The finches were songbirds that he collected from different islands as he travelled around the Galápagos.

Even though the finches looked alike, Darwin saw that there were some big differences between the sizes, beaks and claws of the songbirds. He wanted to know why.

At first, Darwin thought that all the specimens were blackbirds. It was ornithologist John Gould who studied them and revealed that they were actually ground finches. But the really big news was that they were all entirely different species of ground finch.

Darwin began to wonder if each different species had changed so that it could survive on the particular island on which it lived. Big beaks were ideal for eating nuts. Smaller beaks were better for eating insects. It was evidence like this that helped him to come up with an idea that he called natural selection.

Darwin's theory was that species are always changing, little by little.

IN OTHER NEWS

In 1836, Samuel Morse invented the electric telegraph, which was a machine used for sending signals from one town, country or continent, to another. The following year, he invented Morse Code – a language made up of dots and dashes that allowed text messages to be sent by telegraph.

The animals with characteristics best suited to living in their habitat are most likely to survive. These are the animals that go on to have offspring. Those with poorly suited characteristics are less likely to survive. So, it is nature that selects how a species evolves, or changes. The idea that species evolve over time is called evolution.

★ Species ★

A species is a group of living things that are so alike that they can breed together. There can be many different species belonging to one *genus*, or kind, of animal. For example, the tiger, leopard, jaguar and lion species all belong to the genus *panthera*.

WORK, WORK and MORE WORK

Darwin came up with his big idea soon after the voyage of the HMS *Beagle*. But it was to be many years before he published his research. First he wanted to collect a lot of evidence to back up his idea of evolution by natural selection. Darwin didn't tell everyone his idea straight away. He was juggling so many other projects that he didn't have the time.

Darwin was rewriting his journal from the voyage. Once the experts who had examined Darwin's specimens had written their reports, he had to check them, too. These reports would be included in a five-part book he was compiling – *The Zoology of the Voyage of HMS Beagle*. On top of everything else, Darwin wanted to write about geology too.

Darwin had relied on the advice of the experts of many different species while researching natural selection. He decided that he needed to be an expert on at least one species himself. He chose *Cirripedia* – barnacles. Happily, he discovered that the

TRUE or FALSE?

DARWIN SPENT FIVE YEARS STUDYING BARNACLES.

<u>false</u> He actually spent eight years studying these tiny sea creatures.

way barnacles adapt to face new living conditions also provided solid evidence of natural selection. He was awarded the Royal Society's Royal Medal for his scientific work.

Darwin worked so hard that he became very ill. It was while he was recovering from his illness that he met his cousin, Emma Wedgwood, and got to know her better. In January 1839, they were married. But Darwin was never quite well again.

WELL I NEVER!

Charles Darwin drew up a list of advantages and disadvantages before deciding whether or not to ask Emma Wedgwood to marry him. Luckily, there were more advantages and Darwin did propose.

The Darwins first lived in London, before moving to Down House in Kent.

FELLOW PIONEER

In 1858, twenty years after coming up with the idea, Darwin still hadn't finished writing his book about natural selection. Then a naturalist called Alfred Russel Wallace sent Darwin a paper he'd written – about natural selection. Wallace had beaten Darwin to it! Darwin was shocked – but he didn't have the time to correspond with Wallace just then. He had a problem much closer to home.

WHO WAS HE?

FULL NAME: *Alfred Russel Wallace*

DATE OF BIRTH: *8 January 1823*

LIVED: *Wales and England*

JOB: *naturalist*

TOP DISCOVERIES: *natural selection (with Darwin); the Wallace Line (an imaginary line between Australia and south-east Asia – there are different species on either side).*

TOP AWARDS: *Royal Medal; Darwin Medal; Founder's Medal; Linnean Medal; Darwin-Wallace Medal; Order of Merit.*

DIED: *7 November 1913*

In the village where Darwin lived, many children were seriously ill with scarlet fever and he was desperately worried about his own children's health. So he sent Wallace's paper to two scientist friends of his – geologist Charles Lyell and botanist Joseph Hooker – and suggested that Wallace's ideas should be published.

However, Lyell and Hooker decided that the fairest thing to do would be for Darwin and Wallace to make a joint announcement about natural selection.

Carl Linnaeus

Carl ★ Linnaeus ★ (1707–1778)

Linnaeus was a Swedish naturalist, botanist, zoologist and ecologist. He is famous for writing *Systema Naturae*, a book that described a simple system for naming different species. The modern way of naming plants, animals and minerals – binomial nomenclature – is based on Linnaeus' original idea. The Linnean Society of London was named after him.

As they had both independently come up with the same idea, this seemed to be a good solution. The date was set for Darwin and Wallace to present their research on 1 July 1858 at the Linnean Society of London. Sadly, Darwin never made it. His young son – also named Charles – died from scarlet fever just three days before the big day.

Alfred Russel Wallace

ON THE ORIGIN OF SPECIES

In 1859, Charles Darwin's long-awaited book was published. *On the Origin of Species* explained Darwin's ideas on how animal species evolve over time by natural selection. People rushed to buy their copies, and soon everyone was talking about it, not just in the UK but all around the world. However, not everyone agreed with Darwin's ideas.

WHAT HE SAID

As many more individuals of each species are born than can possibly survive ... it follows that any being, if it vary however slightly in any manner profitable to itself ... will have a better chance of surviving, and thus be naturally selected.

On the Origin of Species (1858)

Some members of the Anglican Church were unhappy about Darwin's theory of evolution. It contradicted their religious beliefs about how the Earth and living things were created. Other churchgoers believed that natural selection was all part of God's plan, and so supported Darwin.

The world of science was also divided. Mathematician and astronomer John Herschel said that Darwin's theory was 'higgledy-piggledy'. Darwin's old friends Lyell and Hooker were among those who agreed with Darwin. Within a few years, most scientists had decided that the theory of evolution was true. They just weren't sure if natural selection was the way in which it happened.

On the Origin of Species was not just written for scientists and churchgoers. It was written for the general public, and the book soon became a bestseller.

TRUE or FALSE?

THE FULL TITLE OF DARWIN'S BOOK WAS:
ON THE ORIGIN OF SPECIES BY MEANS OF NATURAL SELECTION, OR THE PRESERVATION OF FAVOURED RACES IN THE STRUGGLE FOR LIFE

true   But as that was a very long title, it was usually shortened to *On the Origin of Species*.

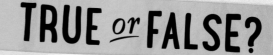

FROM APES to HUMANS

After writing about the evolution of animals, Darwin turned his attention to humans. In 1871, he published another book about evolution. Darwin had already hinted at human evolution in *On the Origin of Species*, but in his new book he tackled it properly. *The Descent of Man* discussed the theory that humans were descended from apes.

Darwin wasn't the first person to write about evolution, but his book got a lot of people talking about the idea. In *The Descent of Man*, Darwin compared humans and animals, to show that they were alike in many ways. He showed that the emotions and thought processes displayed by humans could also be seen in animal species.

Many struggled to believe the idea that humans had evolved from the same ancestor as apes. They thought that humans were so much cleverer than apes that there was no way an ape could share the same evolutionary path. Even Alfred Russel Wallace now sided against Darwin. This upset Darwin very much.

Like Darwin's first book, *The Descent of Man* was also a bestseller. Both books are still in print today.

WELL I NEVER!

Darwin might have discovered and studied many species of animal, but that didn't stop him eating them. While on board the HMS *Beagle*, he feasted upon armadillos and tortoises. He also ate puma, which he said was a little like veal.

IN OTHER NEWS

In 1871, many central European states – some of them smaller than the city of London – joined together. They officially became a new unified empire called Germany, with Kaiser Wilhelm I as the leader. The German Empire lasted just 47 years, until 1918. At the end of World War One, Kaiser Wilhelm II abdicated and the empire became a republic instead.

Kaiser Wilhelm II

Darwin ate armadillos and thought the meat tasted like duck.

25

a GRAND FAREWELL

Darwin was ill for much of his adult life, with a mysterious illness that appeared to be triggered by stress. His poor health meant that he missed many important public events. He spent most of his time at his home in Kent, where his family looked after him while he continued to work.

Although a religious person when he was young, Darwin's studies in evolution changed his mind. He began to question whether the creation of the Earth had happened exactly as it said in the Bible. After much thought and many discussions with his wife Emma, Darwin eventually decided that he was agnostic – he didn't know if God existed or not.

WELL I NEVER!

There are over 120 species named after Darwin, from *Ogcocephalus darwini* (the red-lipped batfish) to *Rhinoderma darwinii* (the southern Darwin's frog).

Darwin died in 1882, aged 73. Although he'd expected to be buried in his own village, he was now far too important for this. Instead, Darwin was given a state funeral and buried at Westminster Abbey in London. Alfred Russel Wallace was one of those who carried his coffin.

WHAT THEY SAID

It would have been unfortunate if anything had occurred to give weight ... to the foolish notion ... that there is a necessary conflict between a knowledge of Nature and a belief in God.

Harvey Goodwin, the Bishop of Carlisle, speaking in Westminster Abbey on the Sunday after Darwin's funeral.

TOP FIVE

Five other famous scientists buried at Westminster Abbey

Sir Isaac Newton (scientist) 1642–1727

Margaret Cavendish, Duchess of Newcastle (scientist) 1661–1717

Charles Lyell (geologist) 1797–1875

Sir J J Thomson (physicist) 1856–1940

Ernest Rutherford (physicist) 1871–1937

AFTER DARWIN

Charles Darwin's theories still cause arguments in the twenty-first century. Although most people believe that his theory of evolution is correct, there are still many others who do not. The theory of evolution is taught in some schools, but not all. It wasn't until the mid-twentieth century that most scientists agreed that natural selection was how evolution worked. It is now generally believed that all life on the Earth has evolved from the same organisms.

Built in 2009, the Darwin Centre is part of the Natural History Museum in London. The highlight of the centre is an enormous cocoon-shaped building. Inside the Cocoon are eight storeys that house millions of insect and plant specimens. Visitors can walk around part of the Cocoon, to see some of the many specimens on display. They can even peek into laboratories to watch actual scientific research happening.

This century, the theory of evolution itself continues to evolve. Scientists are still trying to figure out exactly how the first bacteria, which appeared about 3.5 million years ago, have evolved into the many, many species alive today.

tree

flower

seaweed

WELL I NEVER!

Darwin's sons shone in scientific areas too. George became an astronomer, Francis a botanist and Horace a civil engineer. And all three became Fellows of the Royal Society.

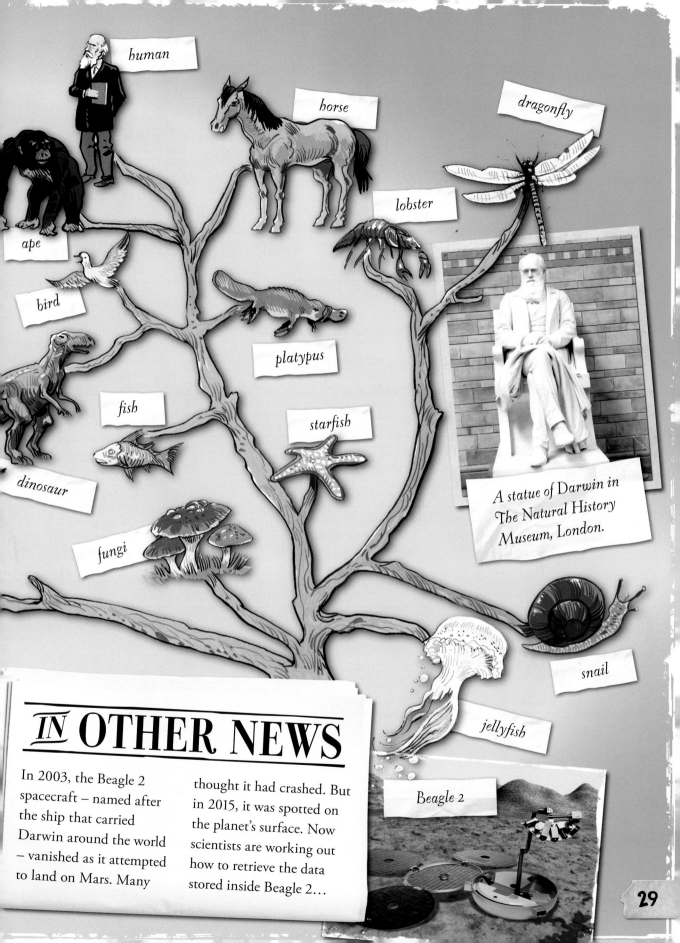

human

horse

dragonfly

ape

lobster

bird

platypus

fish

starfish

dinosaur

A statue of Darwin in The Natural History Museum, London.

fungi

snail

jellyfish

<u>IN</u> OTHER NEWS

In 2003, the Beagle 2 spacecraft – named after the ship that carried Darwin around the world – vanished as it attempted to land on Mars. Many thought it had crashed. But in 2015, it was spotted on the planet's surface. Now scientists are working out how to retrieve the data stored inside Beagle 2…

Beagle 2

1809   Charles Robert Darwin is born.

1817   Darwin's mother dies.

1825   He becomes a medical student at the University of Edinburgh.

1827   He goes to Cambridge University to study theology.

1831   The Voyage of the HMS *Beagle* begins.

1836   The HMS *Beagle* arrives back in the UK.

1837   Darwin presents a paper to the Geological Society of London.

1838   He comes up with his idea of evolution by means of natural selection.

1839   He marries Emma Wedgwood.

1840   *Zoology of the Voyage of the Beagle* is published.

1858   Darwin receives news that Alfred Russel Wallace has also come up with the idea of natural selection.

1858   Darwin's and Wallace's ideas are jointly presented to the Linnaean Society.

1859   *On the Origin of Species* is published.

1871   *The Descent of Man* is published.

1882   Charles Darwin dies.

2009   The Darwin Centre is opened at The Natural History Museum in London, in honour of Charles Darwin.

GLOSSARY

abdicate to give up the throne or power

agnostic someone who can't decide if God exists or not

anaesthetic a drug or gas that means patients don't feel pain during an operation

astronomer a person who studies the stars and planets

bacteria tiny living things

barnacle a sea creature that attaches itself to rocks and ships

botanist someone who studies plants

circumnavigate sail or travel all the way around something

descent where a living thing came from

distinguished important and well regarded by others

evolution the theory that species change over time

evolve to change

expedition a journey or voyage with a purpose

extinct a species that is no longer living

geologist someone who studies our planet: its history; what it is made of and how it is formed

laboratory a place where scientific work is carried out

natural history the study of plants and animals

natural selection the idea that a species changes so that it can adapt to the habitat in which it lives and is better able to survive there

naturalist someone who studies animal and plants

organism the smallest type of living thing, sometimes only a single cell

origin where something comes from or how it begins

ornithologist someone who studies birds

parson someone who leads members of a church in a particular parish or area

philosopher someone who studies really big questions about life

physician a doctor

profitable something that makes money

scarlet fever an infectious disease

species a group of similar living things

specimen an example or a small part of something

surgeon a doctor who is qualified to perform operations

survey to examine and measure an area of land and record the data

zoologist a scientist who studies animals

further information

BOOKS

Scientists who made History: Charles Darwin by Cath Senker (Wayland, 2014)

Who was Charles Darwin? by Deborah Hopkinson (Grosset and Dunlap, 2015)

Evolution Revolution by Robert Winston (DK Children, 2009)

WEBSITES

www.nhm.ac.uk/nature-online/science-of-natural-history/biographies/charles-darwin/
The Natural History Museum's biography and timeline of Charles Darwin.

www.bbc.co.uk/timelines/zq8gcdm
A timeline of Charles Darwin on the BBC website.

PLACES TO VISIT

The Natural History Museum, Cromwell Road, London SW7 5BD

Down House, once Darwin's home, is now open to the public. Luxted Road, Downe, Orpington BR6 7JT

INDEX

More history titles available
from Wayland...

Best and Worst Jobs in...

978 0 7502 8736 4

978 0 7502 8740 1

Truth or Busted

978 0 7502 8129 4

978 0 7502 8130 0

What they don't tell you about...

978 0 7502 8167 6

978 0 7502 8047 1

Awfully Ancient

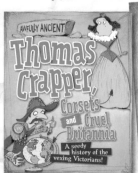

978 0 7502 7991 8

978 0 7502 7987 1

EPIC

978 0 7502 8761 6

978 0 7502 8755 5

Explore!

978 0 7502 8860 6

978 0 7502 9549 9